Bill Adler's
Love Letters
to Elvis

Note:
These letters by Bill Adler reflect the sentiments of Elvis fans around the world. Any one of the letters could have been written by any one of Elvis's thousands of admirers.

Bill Adler's Love Letters to Elvis

GROSSET & DUNLAP
A FILMWAYS COMPANY
Publishers • New York

Other letter books by Bill Adler:

Love Letters to the Beatles
Letters from Camp
Still More Letters from Camp
Kids' Letters to President Kennedy
Dear Senator Kennedy
Love Letters to the Mets
Dear 007
Dear Vet
Hip Kids' Letters from Camp
Dear Shrink
Dear President Johnson
Letters to the Air Force on UFO's
Kids' Letters to the F.B.I.

Copyright © 1978 by Bill Adler Books, Inc.
All rights reserved
Published simultaneously in Canada
Library of Congress catalog card number: 77-94852
ISBN 0-448-14717-3 (hardcover edition)
ISBN 0-448-14733-5 (paperback edition)

First printing 1978
Printed in the United States of America

Bill Adler's Love Letters to Elvis

☆ ☆ ☆

Dear Elvis,

I am writing this letter to you from my bed because I am very sick and I have a 102 degree temperature.

The doctor says I will probably be okay, but now I am very sick!

I can't even eat or drink because I feel so bad and I spend most of the day just sleeping in my bed.

At night I can't sleep so well because I sleep most of the day.

But even though I have 102 degree temperature, I wanted to write to you.

It makes me feel a little better when I think that maybe you will be reading my letter.

Writing a letter to you is better medicine for me than aspirin and cough medicine.

Your sick fan,
Larry G.
U.S.A.

☆ ☆ ☆

☆ ☆ ☆

Dearest Elvis,

I am proud to be an Elvis Presley fan just like I am proud to be an American.

I am proud to be an Elvis Presley fan because I know that Elvis Presley fans believe in Elvis Presley and the American flag.

I know that there are Elvis Presley fans in England, France, Germany, Italy, Japan, Spain and all over the world and they believe in Elvis and their countries too.

Elvis Presley doesn't really belong just to the United States. He belongs to the world.

> *Your fan,*
> Peter L.
> U.S.A.

Dear Elvis Presley,

How do I love you?
Let me count the ways.
I love your smile,
And your beautiful voice.
I love your handsome face.
I love your walk,
And the way you talk.
I love you in millions of ways.
And I love you always for the rest of my days.

Forever,
Diana P.
England

☆ ☆ ☆

Dearest adorable Elvis,

I am thinking you are very sweet.

I am hoping that does not make you blush. I am knowing that boys are not liking to be called sweet, but I cannot help.

I am still thinking you are very sweet.

My many girl friends are thinking you are handsome and I am the only one who is thinking you are sweet.

I am thinking Robert Redford and Paul Newman are sweet too.

All my love,
Sophia T.
Italy

☆ ☆ ☆

Dear Elvis Presley,

There are million questions I want to ask.

There are so many questions I want to ask I cannot know where to begin.

They are questions which to me are important. Only I will ask you the most important questions.

     1. Do you sleep in pajamas or do you sleep in nothing?

     2. Do you brush the teeth after all meals or after breakfast and before sleep?

     3. Do you shave your self or does a barber shave you?

     4. Do you buy you clothes or does the manager buy all your clothes?

     5. Do you sleep on a pillow?

     6. Do you laugh loud or do you chuckle?

     7. What makes you cry or do not you cry because you are a man and men do not cry?

     8. What size shoes do you have?

     9. Do you like to stay up late at night or do you like to get up early in the morning?

     10. Do you like to eat cereal or do you like to eat ham and eggs?

     11. Do you wear undershirt?

     12. Is Coke the favorite drink or do you drink coffee and water?

I hope these questions are not personal, Elvis.

If any of the questions are personal, Elvis, you can cross out and I understand.

> *Very truly,*
> Hans M.
> The Netherlands

P.S. You can write and ask me any questions you want. I answer everything.

☆ ☆ ☆

Dear Elvis,

Your songs are great
And so are you.
There is only one Elvis
But I wish there were two.

A loyal, loving fan,
Marta
The Netherlands

Dear Elvis,

I hope you never grow old, Elvis, because I like you just the way you are.

If you were old like Dean Martin or Frank Sinatra you just wouldn't be the same Elvis.

I know that everybody has to grow old someday, but I hope you don't.

I know you will sing great when you are old and you will probably look good too, but old people just aren't the same as young people.

So please stay young, Elvis, just for me.

Yours,
Mary J.
U.S.A.

☆ ☆ ☆

Dearest Elvis,

My parents don't think I should write to you anymore.

They aren't sure if you are a good influence on me, but I know that you are.

You are my inspiration.

You are the one who makes my days and nights joyous, glorious and divine.

There is no one else who is my inspiration, but you. It is you and only you who makes my days glorious and my nights enchanting and the minutes in between heaven.

Perhaps my parents don't understand what you truly mean to me.

I have tried to explain how I feel to my parents, but I am unable to tell them what is really in my heart and mind.

Maybe someday they will understand.

I hope so because I love my parents and I want to share with them all that you mean to me.

Maybe you could write to my parents or call them on the telephone.

I am sure if they heard your voice, they would fall in love with you too.

Won't you please call?

I can't go on writing these letters after midnight when my parents are asleep.

Your love,
Lois L.
Kansas City

☆ ☆ ☆

☆ ☆ ☆

Dearest Elvis Presley,

I hope you aren't too busy to read our letter.

Marthe and I spent much time trying to think what to say in this letter.

Marthe wanted to write to say that we love you, but I said to her you can't write a letter to Elvis Presley and tell him that you love him when you have not met.

I wanted to write to tell you that I think you are the greatest, but Marthe said that if we wrote to tell you that you were the greatest you would get a swelled head and I said I did not think that because you already know that you are the greatest.

Then Marthe said if we can't write to say to you we love you and if we can't write to say that you are the greatest, what can we write?

Then Marthe found an idea.

"Why don't we write to Elvis to tell him all about ourselves," Marthe said.

I told Marthe that I did not think that a busy superstar like Elvis Presley would have time to read a letter about two twelve-year-old girls from Switzerland.

But if we can't write to tell you that we love you and you are the greatest then what can we write?

Maybe we write and tell you about Marthe and me.

What is there to write besides Marthe and me are very interesting twelve-year-old girls?

You like to hear all about us?

Your fans,
Hedy and Marthe
Switzerland

P.S. We love you and think you are greatest but we cannot write it.

☆ ☆ ☆

☆ ☆ ☆

Dear Elvis Presley,

I am twelve years and I am not yet old to like boys, but I like you.

You are great, Elvis, so that I wish every boy is like you because if they are then I will have liked boys for a long time.

I do not know why I like you, so I ask my big sister Angela.

Angela says that when I will be fifteen years, I will find out why I like you so much.

I hope this because I do not know if I will be able to wait so long.

Your little fan,
Maria R.
Italy

P.S. Angela is seventeen and she likes you and she knows why.

☆ ☆ ☆

☆ ☆ ☆

To Elvis,

Even though you are a big superstar, I know that you are really a regular person just like me and my friends.

That is why I like you so much because I know that you aren't stuck up like some of the other big shot stars in Hollywood.

You are a person who likes to do the same things that ordinary people like to do, like me and my friend, Stanton, and my other friend, Arnie, and his cousin, Randolph.

We like girls and you like girls.

We like music and you like music.

We like to play our guitars and you like to play your guitar.

We like to stay up late at night and you like to stay up late at night.

We like pizza and Brown's soda and you like pizza and Brown's soda.

We like fast cars and you like fast cars.

We like flashy clothes and you like flashy clothes.

We like to sleep late in the morning and you like to sleep late in the morning.

We like grits for breakfast and you like grits for breakfast.

We like to go to the movies a lot and you like to go to the movies a lot.

So you see, Elvis, that is why we like you so much, because you are just a regular person like us except for one thing. You are a millionaire and we are broke.

> *Your admirer,*
> Ralph K.
> San Francisco

Dear Elvis,

Do you believe in love at first sight?

I hope you do because I fell in love with you the first time I saw you on television on the "Ed Sullivan Show," when I was just a kid.

I knew the first time I saw you that you were the only one for me.

There was something about your eyes and the way you walked that sent chills down my spine.

I have seen lots of stars on television since I first saw you on the "Ed Sullivan Show," but nobody has sent chills down my spine except for you.

I guess that is the way it always will be because I doubt if I ever again will see anyone like the Elvis Presley I first saw on the "Ed Sullivan Show."

Frankly, I haven't seen you on television since I saw you on the "Ed Sullivan Show."

Have you changed?

I hope not.

I guess I have changed. I'm not a kid anymore.

> *Love,*
> Denise L.
> Brooklyn

To my beloved Elvis,

I wrote this poem
So you can know
I love you more than I can say
Elvis is the one who means more to me each day!

> *Fondly,*
> Frieda A.
> Germany

P.S. I cannot rhyme the poem so good, but I hope you know that I do love you.

☆ ☆ ☆

Dear Elvis Presley,

If I could talk to you on the telephone here is what I would say:

"Hello Elvis, this is Sandra, in the Bronx."

"How are you Elvis? I hope you aren't working too hard."

"What are you doing right now, Elvis?"

"Oh, that's right, right now you are talking to me on the telephone. What will you be doing tomorrow?"

"Perhaps if you aren't too busy tomorrow, Elvis, we could talk on the telephone again tomorrow."

"I guess you know why I called you, Elvis."

"To tell you the truth, Elvis, I sort of have a crush on you."

"I hope you aren't blushing because I have told you that over the telephone, Elvis."

"I guess I could have told you that I have a crush on you in a letter, but I wanted to say it with my own voice."

"I was wondering, Elvis, since we are just chatting here on the telephone like old friends, perhaps you could sing a little tune for me. Any tune will be all right. I just get goose pimples at the sound of your voice."

"By the way, Elvis, I am paying for the phone call so we can talk as long as you want."

Well, Elvis, that's what I would say to you if we were talking on the phone except for one thing.

I wouldn't pay for the call. I can't even afford to call Brooklyn and I live in the Bronx.

Your fan,
Sandra T.
The Bronx

☆ ☆ ☆

To my wonderful Elvis,

How can I tell you I love you when I do not know you? But I want very much to tell you I love you anyway, because there is something inside me that says I love you very, very much.

I wish I am a great writer so I have the right words to tell you I love you, but if I try very hard, the right words do not come from my heart to my pen.

Perhaps someday I will find the right words.

When I will, I will send you another letter to say I love you. But I hope you will read this letter and will imagine that I have the right words.

> *Forever my love,*
> Christina M.
> Denmark

Dearest Elvis,

This little poem is for you.
It comes from my soul and I hope you like it.
Here is my poem:
Someday we will walk hand and hand,
For the whole world to see.
Then the whole world will know
That Elvis Presley is the one for me.
I hope you liked my poem.

> *Love from,*
> Gerda M.
> Germany

P.S. Please do not show this poem to any one because it is for you.

Dearest Elvis,

My boyfriend and I fight over you all the time.

My boyfriend is jealous of you and he says that I am really in love with you and not with him.

It's not true.

I am in love with him, but I am also in love with you.

I love you each for different reasons.

I love my boyfriend (his name is Thomas) because we like to do things together like go to the school football games and to Sally's Pizza Place after the game.

We always go dutch because Thomas is always broke, but I love him anyway.

I love you, Elvis, because you are the most exciting man in the whole world.

I know that there could never be anything between us and I keep telling that to Thomas, but he doesn't believe me.

He is sure that someday you and I will be together.

I will go on loving you always, Elvis, but it would be a big help if you would write to Thomas and tell him that I'm not your type.

Love always and forever,
Cynthia K.
U.S.A.

☆ ☆ ☆

Dear Elvis,

You are causing a serious problem with my life.

The problem is every time I meet a boy, I make the comparison of the boy to you and I have not met a boy who is close to you.

My friends tell me that it is ridiculous because when I date a boy only one time, I drop him because he is not Elvis.

"You will never find anybody like Elvis," my best friend is saying.

Last week I thought I met a boy who changed all that.

His name was Robert and he was very tall and very clever and very handsome.

I thought that I was in love with Robert, but I began to think, "He is not as good as Elvis," and this is when I end my relationship with Robert.

My friends are saying that I have a very serious problem because I am dreaming of the perfect man like Elvis Presley.

I hope that is not true.

There must be another Elvis Presley somewhere in the world for me because if there isn't, I will become an old maid.

Love,
Jeanne M.
France

☆ ☆ ☆

Dear Elvis, the man I adore!

I thought you would like to know what my favorite Elvis Presley records are.

Here they are:

"Jailhouse Rock"
"Hard-Headed Woman"
"I Got Stung"
"A Fool Such as I"
"A Big Hunk of Love"
"Love Me Tender"
"I Want You, I Love You"
"Hound Dog"
"Too Much"
"All Shook Up"
"Loving You"

I will send you a list tomorrow of my second favorite Elvis Presley records and the next day I will send you a list of my third favorite Elvis Presley records.

I will keep sending you a list until I run out of favorite Elvis Presley records even if it takes me the rest of my life.

Yours forever,
Lorraine H.
Tuscaloosa

☆ ☆ ☆

My darling Elvis,

If I have one wish in the world, that wish is to pass five minutes with you alone somewhere where there is no one but you and me.

That is my one wish.

I am not wishing for a new automobile or a million francs or a journey to London or Paris.

I wish only to be with you alone so I can touch your hands and look in your eyes and caress your hair.

That is my only wish and if that wish will be granted, I will not wish again in my life as long as I will live.

Everything I want is only five minutes with you.

Do you think my wish is too demanding?

> *Thousand kisses,*
> Michelle G.
> Lyons, France

P.S. I know in my heart that my wish will not come true, but the little Michelle will dream and hope that perhaps there will be a miracle and my wish will happen.

This will be the most glorious day of my life.

☆ ☆ ☆

Dear Elvis Presley,

You are the most handsome man I have ever seen on television, in the movies, or in real life.

I think I know why you are the most handsome man.

It is because you are such a beautiful person inside.

I can look in your eyes and know that you are kind and gentle and nice.

If there are more beautiful people in the world like you, Elvis, there will never be any more wars or hate in the world.

That is why I am writing to you, Elvis.

I want you to know how you are beautiful.

I hope you will not get proud because you are the most beautiful person, because beautiful people are usually not proud.

> *Love forever,*
> Yumi G.
> Japan

☆ ☆ ☆

Dear Elvis,

Do you believe in ESP? I believe in ESP because every now and then I believe I know what you are thinking, even though you are thousands of miles away.

Sometimes, I know you are thinking about your singing, and sometimes my ESP tells me that you are thinking about your little baby, and sometimes my ESP tells me that you are thinking about relaxing and fishing, and sometimes my ESP tells me that you are thinking about your fans.

The only sad thing about my ESP is that I never have feelings that you are thinking about me.

> *Your fan,*
> Pauline K.
> Poland

My darling Elvis,

What can I do to make you happy?

Anything you want, I will do.

I have dedicated my life to you and to your happiness.

I want you to be happy all the time, even when you are sleeping or you have the flu or a headache or a stomachache.

> *Your fan,*
> Bridie L.
> Ireland

☆ ☆ ☆

To my darling Elvis,

I hope you won't think I am rude for writing this letter.

Perhaps you will think that what I am writing is none of my business, but I am going to write it anyway.

Here is what I have to say Elvis.

I think you have been working too hard. Yesterday, I saw your picture in the newspaper and you looked very tired to me.

Why do you have to work so hard, Elvis?

It isn't fair to all your fans who don't want to see you look so tired.

Maybe you should go on a vacation, Elvis, so you won't be so tired.

I hope you are not mad at me for writing this letter, Elvis, but I am worried about you and I want you to stay young and healthy and that is why I worry when you look tired.

Of course, I am not a doctor, but I once read an article in *Seventeen* magazine about how to take care of yourself, so I am sort of an expert.

> Susan W.
> U.S.A.

☆ ☆ ☆

Dear Elvis,

This is the first love letter I have ever written in my whole life and I am writing it to you.

I don't even know how to begin a real love letter.

Do I tell you right away how much I love you, or do I talk about the weather first?

Should I tell you why I love you, or should I just hint and let you guess?

How mushy and romantic should I get in a love letter?

Should I pour out my heart and tell you how I really feel?

I wish I had written a love letter before so I would know how to do it.

I asked my best friend, Oona, to help, but she has never written a love letter either.

I suppose I will just have to do my best.

I hope this love letter isn't too awkward or embarrassing, Elvis.

Please remember that it is my very first love letter and after I get some practice, I will be much better.

Anyway, what I really wanted to say in my first love letter is "Elvis, I love you."

> *Yours forever,*
> Dora B.
> Ireland

☆ ☆ ☆

☆ ☆ ☆

Dearest Elvis,

I would like to ask you a very personal question which I hope you will answer for me.

What is your idea of the perfect woman?

Is she tall or short?

Does she have blue, black, or hazel eyes?

Is she thin?

Is her hair long or short, blond, brown, black, or red?

Does she have a Southern accent, a New England accent, a Midwestern accent, or a New York accent?

Does she like *only* rock and roll music or does she like classical music and opera and hillbilly music?

What are her favorite foods?

Does she like steak, hamburger, hot dogs, pizza, or chinese food?

What sort of clothes does she wear?

Is she always wearing jeans or does she wear dresses and shorts?

I would really like to know what is your idea of the perfect woman and then I will pray that maybe it is me.

> *Love forever,*
> Doris J.
> U.S.A.

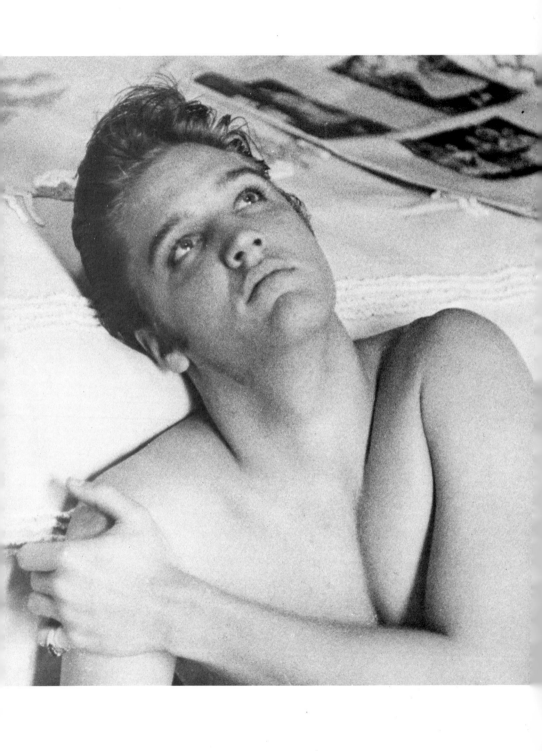

☆ ☆ ☆

To Elvis,

Do you need somebody to take care of you? Somebody to cook meals and mend socks and sew buttons on your shirt and make your bed and clean your room and shop for you?

Dear Elvis, this somebody could be me.

I am not the best cook in the world and I do not know how to sew so good, but I can learn.

I will like to take care of you and I will take especially care of you when you do not feel good.

Someday I hope to be a nurse so I will like to practice by taking care of you.

I know what to do when you have a cold. I will give you two aspirins.

I know what to do when you have a headache. I will give you two aspirins.

I know what to do if you have the flu. I will give you two aspirins.

May I come and take care of you?

Love,
Wilma G.
Sweden

P.S. I will bring my aspirin.

☆ ☆ ☆

☆ ☆ ☆

Dear Elvis,

Do you think that your fantastic manager, Colonel Parker, will like to manage me?

I am thirteen years old and someday I am going to be a rock and roll superstar.

I am reading in the newspaper that your manager, Colonel Parker, is the best manager in the world. This is why I like him to be my manager too.

How much does your manager cost to make me a superstar?

I cannot spend great money to be a superstar, but when I become a superstar, I will pay him all the money I owe.

Do you have a contract with your manager, Colonel Parker, or do you just shake hands?

I will like to meet Colonel Parker to discuss my future.

Do not worry. I will not be a superstar before you are retired or nobody ever heard of you anymore.

> *Your fan the future
> superstar,*
> Martino G.
> Italy

☆ ☆ ☆

Dear darling, wonderful Elvis,

I want to hold your hand and stroke your hair and touch your lips.

I thank the Lord that I am alive when Elvis is king.

How terrible it would be to be alive when there is no Elvis and there are no Elvis Presley records to listen to or Elvis Presley movies to see.

I would not want to live then because life would not be the same.

The world is a more beautiful and more wonderful place today because there is Elvis Presley and we can listen to his glorious music and look at his wonderful face and watch his lovely movements.

I owe it all to my parents.

If they had not had me, I would not have know how wonderful life can be when there is a world with Elvis Presley.

All my love,
Isabella R.
Brazil

☆ ☆ ☆

To the one and only Elvis,

When is your birthday?

Do you know your Zodiac sign?

Is it Leo or Capricorn?

I am a Leo, so I hope you are a Leo too.

It would be super, super if we are the same sign, but if we are not, I will not be angry.

You will still be the one only Elvis for me even if you were born to have the wrong sign.

Love and kisses,
Angela C.
Argentina

P.S. It was not your fault when you were born. It was your parents'.

Dear Elvis Presley,

My girlfriend, Annie, and I argue about you all the time.

We argue about who is a better Elvis Presley fan, she or me.

Annie has sixty-two Elvis Presley records and I have sixty-four Elvis Presley records, but I have twenty-eight Elvis Presley pictures and Annie has twenty-six Elvis Presley pictures.

I have seen every Elvis Presley movie two times and Annie has seen every Elvis Presley picture three times.

Annie has seen six Elvis Presley concerts and I have seen four Elvis Presley concerts because I did not have money to buy tickets to the other two Elvis Presley concerts.

I have written thrity-four fan letters to you and Annie has written thirty-four fan letters to you.

I have seven Elvis Presley T-shirts and Annie has five Elvis Presley T-shirts, but she only wears three of them.

I think of you all the time and Annie says she thinks of you all the time.

Annie is president of our Elvis Presley Fan Club this year and I was president of our Elvis Presley Fan Club last year.

Who do you think is a better Elvis Presley fan? Annie or me?

I hope you write to me to tell me what you think.

If you think Annie is a better Elvis Presley fan, do not answer this letter.

Fondly,
Olga G.
Denmark

Dear Elvis Presley,

Are you ever lonely?

I am lonely all the time, that is why I am writing to you.

When I am lonely, the only person I want to be with is Elvis Presley because I know that you really understand lonely people like me.

Do you think I could come and see you when I am lonely, Elvis?

I would come to your house and sit quietly for a few minutes and then I would leave.

It isn't any fun to be lonely.

I have lots of friends and relatives and I even have a dog, but I am still lonely.

I hope you will say yes, Elvis, because I don't want to be lonely for the rest of my life.

Lonely people are very sad.

Your fan,
Roger S.
U.S.A.

☆ ☆ ☆

Dear Elvis, the greatest star!

I have wanted to write to you since I have heard your first record five years ago, but I did not know what I will say to you if I ever wrote to you so that is why for five years I have waited.

Now I think I know what I want to write to you. It was this.

Do the words of the songs you sing have a hidden meaning? Are you trying to tell us something?

For five years I have listened to your records and I am still trying to find out.

Your friend,
Wilhelm G.
Germany

☆ ☆ ☆

Dearest Elvis,

I almost did a foolish, impulsive thing.

I was at the hotel where you were appearing in Las Vegas and I was sitting at a table very close to the stage—so close that I almost thought I could reach out and touch you.

While you were singing your last song, I had a sudden uncontrollable urge to reach out and touch you.

Just as I was about to stretch out my hand to touch you, a voice within me said, "Don't do it."

I listened to that voice and I didn't touch you, but now I am sorry that I didn't reach out to touch you because I will probably never have a chance to touch you again.

That is why I am writing to you.

Could you please tell me when you will be appearing in Las Vegas again?

I would like one more chance to reach out and touch you.

Your fan,
Phyllis K.
San Francisco

☆ ☆ ☆

☆ ☆ ☆

Dearest Elvis Presley,

It is foolish and stupid for me to be in love with you because we have never met and you do not know me.

Even though I have never met you, I feel as though I know you all my life and that is why I love you.

You do not have to be with a person to love him and though I have not been with you, I love you.

Why do I love you?

There are many reasons.

You are someone very special and when you smile that wonderful warm smile, I feel you are smiling for me.

I love you because you are a beautiful person. Maybe you are not the most handsome person in the world, but you look perfect for me.

I do not love you because you are rich and famous. I love you even if you were poor and nobody.

Love is not easy to explain because love is a feeling that is coming from inside a person.

Love is knowing you wish to make the other happy and that you wish to do things for the other.

I have no right to love you, dear Elvis, but I cannot prevent it.

My love for you is so strong that if I did not write to tell you it, I can never be honest with myself.

Now you know what I feel.

I do not wait for you to write to say that you love me also. This is more than I can expect.

But I will continue loving you because nothing can change my love for you even when I get married sometime.

My husband must understand.

> *Forever yours,*
> Leonora J.
> Brazil

Dear Elvis,

This is the first letter I am writing to you, but now that I have written to you I will write to you every day for the rest of my life.

Every night before I sleep, I will write to you and tell you everything I did during the day from the minute I got up in the morning until the minute I go to bed at night.

I want you to know everything about Bettina because Bettina is very interesting.

Maybe when you receive my letters, you will want to meet me.

> *Your fan,*
> Bettina L.
> Belgium

☆ ☆ ☆

Darling Elvis,

If I could only touch you—if only for a second. It would mean so much to me because you are my idol and for me there is no other man who means as much to me.

I know it is foolish on my part to think that someday we might be married, but still I like to think those sweet, wonderful thoughts.

Imagine, Brenda ———, Mrs. Elvis Presley.

It could never happen because you have never met me and even though I was voted the prettiest girl in my class, there are many other beautiful women who would give anything to be Mrs. Elvis Presley.

So what chance does poor Brenda ——— have?

But I can still dream and hope because all I want in the world is to become Mrs. Elvis Presley.

Even if it was only for a day.

> *Love forever,*
> Brenda C.
> U.S.A.

☆ ☆ ☆

Darling Elvis,

I want to do something nice for you because you have brought so much joy to me and the rest of the world.

What can I do for you, dear Elvis?

Can I bake you a cake or knit you a sweater or buy something nice for you? Anything you want.

Of course, I don't have much money because I don't get a very big allowance, but I will try to buy whatever will make you happy.

Nobody has made me as happy as you have, Elvis, and I want to do something in return.

Please write to me and tell me what I can do.

Even if you don't have time to write me a long letter to tell me what you would like, maybe you could send me a postcard with the name of the gift you would like.

I really want to please you, even if I have to spend my last peso.

With all my love,
Lola F.
Mexico

Dear Elvis,

Last week I took the entire week and painted this picture of you.

I really truly hope you like it.

I am not really a professional artist and I don't have all the equipment that a professional has, but I did the best I could.

Maybe if you like this small painting of you, you will pose for me someday so I can paint a better picture of you.

It is very hard to paint a picture of someone from just a newspaper photograph.

If you would pose for me, I would buy some real artist's material so I could paint the best possible picture of you.

I would give you the painting when I finish it, if you would pose for me, even if the painting belonged in a museum.

> *Love from a fan,*
> Catherine B.
> England

☆ ☆ ☆

Dear Elvis Presley,

I have tried not to love you because I know that you can never love me back, but no matter how hard I try, I just can't stop loving you.

Maybe someday, I will find somebody to take your place, but until I do, you will have my heart and mind and soul and love.

I have nothing else to give you.

> *Kisses from,*
> Victoria P.
> England

Dear Elvis,

I told my mother that I love you and she said that I would get over it when I get older.

I told my father that I love you and he said that you are too old for me.

I don't think you are too old for me and I don't think I will get over you when I get older.

I am sixteen years old so I am practically older already.

And I don't think you are too old for me because we have a lot in common.

We both like Elvis Presley records and you were born in Memphis and I once rode through Memphis on a Greyhound bus.

> *Love forever,*
> Gilda L.
> U.S.A.

Dear Elvis,

I have tried to keep a secret my love for you, but I do not think I can keep it a secret any longer.

Now I do not care who knows I feel for you.

I was afraid if everybody knew how much I love you, they will laugh at me. Now I want them all to know.

My love for you is real and genuine and it is love that I never have felt for anyone else and I know I never will feel for anyone again.

I have tried to keep it a secret since I have known I love you, but it is a too strong feeling to keep a secret.

It has been since two days I knew I love you and the whole world knows.

> *Forever my love,*
> Louisa P.
> Spain

☆ ☆ ☆

To my favorite, Elvis,

I was only two years old when I heard my first Elvis Presley record and I have been an Elvis Presley fan ever since.

Even when I was only two I knew that there was only one singer for me and that singer was Elvis Presley.

By the time I was six, I had my own collection of Elvis Presley records and while all the other girls were playing with dolls, I was listening to Elvis records.

I used to bring my Elvis Presley records and my Elvis pictures to my kindergarten class and play the records for my friends and show the pictures to my teacher.

When I was eight, I had every single Elvis Presley record and I had thirty-two different pictures of Elvis. I even started on an Elvis Presley scrapbook and every day I would put another story about Elvis in my scrapbook.

Now I am sixteen and I still am an Elvis Presley fan even though I am getting pretty old.

I guess I will always be an Elvis Presley fan even though I am not really a kid anymore.

Bea M.
U.S.A.

☆ ☆ ☆

✩ ✩ ✩

Dear, darling, dearest Elvis,

I think of you all the day also when I have something else to think.

You are always in my mind from the first moment when I wake in the morning to the last moment I fall asleep at night.

I think of you when I am riding on the school bus, when I am eating my lunch and dinner, and when I am watching television.

I think of you when I am in the history class and when I am doing the mathematics at home.

I think of you when I am brushing my teeth and when I am bathing.

I think of you when I am riding my bicycle and when I am shopping in the market.

There is never a moment, or any hour of any day, when I not think of you.

This is why my life is so beautiful.

Always I am thinking of you.

> *Your loving fan,*
> Risa G.
> Spain

Dear Elvis,

There is no night without my dreaming of you.

Last night I dreamed that you and I together danced all night.

The night before last night, I dreamed that you and I together were on a magnificent moonlight cruise to Morocco.

One time I dreamed that you invited me to your house for the weekend and it was only you and me together and your dogs and we listened to Elvis Presley records all weekend.

Each night before I sleep, dear Elvis, I wonder what I will dream of Elvis Presley tonight.

I am the most lucky girl in the world because I dream of Elvis Presley. Other people are not so lucky as me because they do not dream of Elvis.

Mama says that when she comes into my room to look while I am sleeping, I am always smiling.

> Maria J.
> Spain

Dear beloved Elvis,

I love you more every day
I love you more in every way
I love you more and that's the truth
No one loves you more than your fan Ruth

> *Forever,*
> Ruth G.
> Dallas

☆ ☆ ☆

Dearest Elvis,

I wish I can be with you so we can be together alone.

I wish I can be with you so I can put my arms around you and hold you close to me.

I wish I can be with you so we can talk until dawn about you and your life and your hopes and your dreams.

I wish I can be with you so I can tell you how much you mean to me now and how much you mean to me tomorrow and tomorrow and tomorrow.

I wish I can be with you alone so I can caress your hair.

I wish I can be with you so I can watch you walk and talk and eat and smile.

I wish I can be alone with you. Just you and me, so that I can tell you how much you mean and the reason my life is not be worth living without you.

I wish I can be with you twenty-four hours in a day, seven days in a week, forever and forever.

I wish I can be with you so we can sit together at the side of the fire to listen to your records.

I wish I can be with you so you can sing softly for me after we listened to your records.

I wish I can be with you and maybe someday I can because maybe if I wish enough, my wish can come true.

Love and kisses,
Lara K.
Poland

Dear Elvis,

My cat, Tabby, just had four kittens and I would like to know if you would like to have one of the kittens for your very own.

The kittens are very cute and loveable and I would like you to have the cutest and most loveable kitten just for yourself.

Do you like kittens?

I hope you do because kittens are sweet and loveable and they will love you, too.

I'll bet a lot of your fans love kittens, Elvis, and that is why I would like to give you one of my kittens.

When your fans find out that you have a kitten you will even be more popular than you are now.

Love,
Jennifer W.
U.S.A.

☆ ☆ ☆

Dearest Elvis,

Someday my prince will come,
I know that is true.
But even when my prince does come,
My truest love in the world will be only you!

Love,
Doris F.
England

Darling Elvis,

I want to hold your hand and whisper in your ear and dance all night with you.

I know that sounds like a dream by some starry-eyed teenager, but that is how I feel and I don't care if it sounds foolish.

I don't ask for much. I don't want to have you forever. I know that can never be.

But why can't I hold your hand and whisper sweet thoughts in your ear and dance away the night and day?

Please help me make my dream come true.

I will be grateful to you for the rest of my days.

> *Love and kisses,*
> Darlene K.
> England

☆ ☆ ☆

My dear, wonderful, darling, adorable, sweet, marvelous Elvis,

I cannot live without you.

The thought of being without you sends me into a deep depression.

Why can I not be with you always?

Where you are, I want to be.

If you are in London, I want to be in London.

If you are in Tokyo, I want to be in Tokyo.

If you are in Las Vegas, I want to be in Las Vegas.

Please take me with you.

I am only four feet ten inches and I don't need much room.

> *Your loyal fan,*
> Constance L.
> Italy

Dear Elvis Presley,

My girlfriend, Tanga, made me an Elvis Presley doll.

It almost looks like you, but, of course, it isn't real.

Some days I sit in my room all alone and talk to my Elvis Presley doll.

I tell my Elvis Presley doll how much I love it, but my Elvis Presley doll can't tell me back that it loves me.

I wish the real Elvis Presley could tell me that he loves me.

I am tired of talking to a doll.

> *Love and kisses,*
> Victoria H.
> Australia

☆ ☆ ☆

Dear Elvis, the king,

Every morning when I wake, the first thing I do is to kiss the big picture of Elvis Presley in my room.

Every day before I go to school, I kiss the big picture of Elvis Presley in my room.

Every night before I sleep I kiss the big picture of Elvis Presley in my room.

Sometimes I kiss the big picture of Elvis Presley in my room when I suddenly want to.

Yesterday, I have kissed the big picture of Elvis Presley in my room twenty-three times.

> *Your loving fan,*
> Veronique K.
> Germany

☆ ☆ ☆

Dearest Elvis Presley,

Do you think I should wear my hair short?

My mother thinks I should and my best friend, Beth, thinks I should wear my hair short and so does my ex-boyfriend, Billy.

But before I cut my hair short, I want to make sure you will like my hair short.

I am sending you a picture of me with my hair long so you can see what I look like with long hair.

Do you like my hair long or would you like it better short?

I want to please my mother and my girlfriend, but most of all I want to please you, Elvis.

Please write to me and tell me what you think because I don't want to cut my hair short if you don't want me to.

Love,
Sherri W.
U.S.A.

P.S. I don't care what my ex-boyfriend thinks.

☆ ☆ ☆

☆ ☆ ☆

Dear Elvis,

I hope you won't consider this letter to be too romantic, but I do have warm loving feelings about you, although I know you don't have the same feelings about me because you have never met me.

But even though I have never met you in person, Elvis, I feel as though I have known you all my life.

I can never think of a day when I haven't awakened in the morning with that warm, wonderful feeling that it was going to be another glorious day when I could look at the Elvis Presley colour picture hanging in my room and spend the rest of the day listening to the 125 Elvis Presley records I have in my room.

I hope you won't think this letter is too romantic, Elvis, but I wanted you to know how I feel about you because my life has been made brighter and happier because there is an Elvis Presley.

Love,
Gwendolyn G.
England

☆ ☆ ☆

☆ ☆ ☆

Dearest Elvis Presley,

I wish I could write to tell you that which is in my heart, but even if I try hard, the right words do not come.

When you feel for someone the way I feel for you, it is not easy to say it the way to want to say it.

Your records and your music and your movies mean much to me.

When I have a bad day at the school or my parents or my friends give me problems, I play always one of your records and my problems go away.

You are very important in my life and I am afraid that if I did not have Elvis records to cheer me, I would be very unhappy much of the time.

This is the reason it is difficult to tell you that which is in my heart because you only can fill my heart with love and happiness.

> *Kisses from*
> Gianna L.
> Italy

☆ ☆ ☆

To my dear Elvis,

Whenever I want to get away from my troubles, I sit quietly in my room and listen to one of your records.

Somehow, after I listen to your voice, I feel much better.

I almost feel as if you have been singing only for me, but, of course, I know that isn't true.

Still your songs do something for me. They lift my spirits and always put me in a good mood.

I feel as if I have no trouble after I listen to you.

If everybody in the world would listen to Elvis Presley records, the world would be a much happier place because you would make everybody happy like you do me.

> *Your friend,*
> Douglas H.
> Scotland

Dearest Elvis dear,

How can one man be so gorgeous as you?

You are perfect.

Each part of your beautiful face and your magnificent body is a sight to behold.

If you were not perfect, you would still be king, the one only Elvis Presley.

There never has been a man as perfect as you before you and there never will be a man as perfect as you after you.

> *Love forever,*
> Lucia L.
> Italy

Dear sweet Elvis,

I have always dreamed that someday my Prince Charming will come and sweep me off my feet.

You are the Prince Charming I have always dreamed, Elvis.

You are my Prince Charming on a white horse with shining armor.

You are the Prince Charming in my dreams who will take me to an enchanted land where we will live happily ever after.

Will you be my Prince Charming, Elvis?

Can you be my Prince Charming, Elvis?

I know that there are thousands and thousands and thousands of girls who have dreamed like me that someday their Prince Charming will come, but my Prince Charming has to be very special.

That is why my Prince Charming can only be you.

> *All my love,*
> Arlette K.
> Belgium

Dear Elvis P.,

Someday when I am old and gray,
I will think back and remember the day,
When I wrote the poem to Elvis the king,
The only one who really turns me on when I hear
  him sing.

> *Your secret fan,*
> Rebecca W.
> San Diego

☆ ☆ ☆

Dear Elvis Presley,

Your parents must be very proud of you.

I'll bet they never dreamed when you were born that their little son, Elvis, would become the greatest superstar of them all.

My parents are proud of me too. I am president of my class and I am the best basketball player in my school, but I am not a superstar like you.

When did your parents first know that you would be a superstar?

Did you have a great singing voice when you were just a kid? Or did you become a superstar when you were in high school or did it happen after you left high school?

Maybe I'll be a superstar after I get out of high school so my parents will even be prouder of me than they are now.

But even if I am not a superstar, I know that they will always love me anyways.

> *Your friend,*
> Glenn K.
> U.S.A.

Dear Elvis,

I know you can have any girl in the world you want. Why will you consider me? I am not beautiful and I have never appeared in films or on television and I am not a very good singer.

Why me?

What do I offer you, darling Elvis?

Only my love.

My total, complete, individual love I can give you.

I hope this is enough because this is all I have.

> *Forever yours,*
> Katrina F.
> Holland

P.S. My total love is better than anybody else's total love.

☆ ☆ ☆

Dearest Elvis Presley,

Do you get nervous before you go on the stage?

You do not seem to be nervous at all. You seem always relaxed when you are performing.

How do you not get nervous?

Did you get nervous when you first started to sing?

I read in the newspaper that many stars get nervous before they go on the stage, but I suppose you do not get nervous because you are a super star.

> *Your truly,*
> Rolf H.
> Germany

Darling Elvis,

I have wanted to write a love song for you, but I could not do it.

I have tried and tried and tried, but the words and music just would not come.

How can I set to music and words the love and warmth and tenderness that I feel for you?

How can I set to words and music the joy I feel when I hear your voice?

How can I set to words and music the inspiration you give to your millions of fans?

How can I set to words and music what you mean to me?

I cannot.

This is why I have decided to write this letter.

> *Love,*
> Sonja P.
> Poland

☆ ☆ ☆

Dear Elvis,

I have written to the President of the United States and I have asked him to make your birthday a national holiday like Washington's birthday, Lincoln's birthday, Veterans' Day, and Mother's Day.

I hope that the President will make your birthday a national holiday because you are the most popular person in the United States except for maybe Captain Kangaroo.

> *Your fan,*
> Stanley W.
> U.S.A.

☆ ☆ ☆

Dear Elvis,

It has taken me three years to get up the courage to write to you, and now that I am writing to you I don't know exactly what to say.

Should I tell you how much I love you or why I think you are the greatest singer that ever lived?

Should I tell you that I listen to your records all the time and that my favorite Elvis Presley record is "Hound Dog?"

Should I tell you that I have seen all the Elvis Presley movies and that my favorite Elvis Presley movie is *King Creole*?

Should I tell you that I have a six-foot color picture of Elvis Presley hanging over my bed?

Should I tell you that once I saw you in person at an Elvis Presley concert and it was way out?

Should I tell you that I dream about you every night and sometimes I dream about you even when I am not sleeping?

Should I tell you that I never loved another singer like I love you? Not even the Beatles or John Denver or Tom Jones or the Rolling Stones.

Should I tell you that I belong to six Elvis Presley Fan Clubs and that next week I am going to join three more Elvis Presley Fan Clubs?

You see, Elvis, now that I am finally writing to you, I don't know exactly what to say.

Love and kisses,
Esther W.
U.S.A.

Dearly beloved Elvis,

There is magic in your songs.
There is magic in your voice.
And that is why, dear Elvis,
That you, above all, are the people's choice.

Fondly,
Sylvia G.
Louisville

☆ ☆ ☆

Dear Elvis,

You have a lot of sex appeal.

I bet there isn't another man in the whole world who has as much sex appeal as you except maybe Prince Charles. I think he has a lot of sex appeal too, but Prince Charles can't sing and he doesn't give concerts or make records.

But I have to admit, Prince Charles does have a lot of sex appeal. He has an adorable smile and I think it is sweet the way he walks with his hands behind his back.

Even though I do think that Prince Charles of England has a lot of sex appeal, I still don't think he has as much sex appeal as you.

Maybe you won't ever be the King of England, but now you are the king to your millions of fans around the world.

Hail, hail to Elvis Presley.

Your loyal subject,
Bernice K.
England

Dearly beloved Elvis,

I would like very much to buy you a shirt.

Could you please send me your shirt size?

I want to buy you a good shirt at the best store in Detroit. I don't care how much it costs.

The reason I want to buy you a shirt is that the next time you are on television, I want you to wear my shirt so I can tell my friends, "Watch Elvis on television. He is wearing my shirt."

Please send me your shirt size as soon as possible.

> *Your fan,*
> Arnold G.
> Detroit

P.S. What color shirt do you like? Red, green, blue, brown, or purple?

☆ ☆ ☆

Dear Elvis,

I have bought 365 greeting cards so that I can send you a different greeting card every day for the year so that you will know every day that Anya is thinking of Elvis Presley every day in the year.

365 days I love you.

> Anya P.
> Poland

Dear Elvis,

I hope and pray every day that you are very happy because you have bringed so much happiness to millions of people in all the world.

You make people happy when you sing or act or talk.

I wish I will be able make people happy the way you do, but I suppose the only one I make happy is my little dog, Frieda.

Helga L.
Germany

☆ ☆ ☆

Dear Elvis,

My parents just have bought me a new puppy.

The puppy is very small and very sweet with sad eyes and a funny bark.

I love my new puppy very much because I have wanted always a puppy and now I have one.

I almost love my new little puppy as much as I love you.

I did not know what to call my new puppy's name until I thought I would like to name him Elvis, for you.

Will you mind if I named my new puppy Elvis after you.

Will you mind if I named my new puppy Elvis after you even though he is a mongrel?

Jan P.
Sweden

Dear Elvis,

I wish to be shipwrecked on a desert island with you so that I can spend the rest of my life being alone with you without any of your screaming fans.

I will cook for you and make your clothes and sing for you when you are tired from singing for yourself and I will make you very happy.

Will you like to be shipwrecked on a desert island with me, Elvis?

> *Your fan,*
> Ruth G.
> Poland

☆ ☆ ☆

To my sweet Elvis,

I have a very unusual request.

Please send me one of your pillow cases.

I want to put it over my pillow so that I can sleep on your pillow case.

I imagine me resting my head on the same pillow case that Elvis Presley has rested his head on.

I will sleep more well every night when I know that I am sleeping on Elvis Presley's pillow case.

If you cannot send me a pillow case, perhaps you can send me a washcloth or maybe some soap.

Anything that Elvis Presley has touched!

> *I love you!*
> Julia E.
> Belgium

Darling Elvis,

Do you remember the last letter in which I said I love you?

It was the letter from Paris that smelled from Chanel No. 5 perfume and was closed with a kiss. Now do you remember?

Well, darling Elvis, I am writing to you again to tell you that I love you more than I did when I wrote you my last letter.

My love for you grows every minute of every day.

I am sure that when I write you the next time, my love for you will even be more than it is today, which is more than it was last week!

> *Thousand kisses,*
> Francine G.
> Paris

My dear Elvis,

You have the most beautiful eyes and mouth and most wonderful nose in the whole world.

I would like to write and say that you are perfect, but my mother says that nobody is really perfect, not even my father or the President of the United States.

But if there ever was a perfect man, Elvis, I know it would be you.

> *Your loving fan,*
> Mary Ann L.
> U.S.A.

Dear Elvis,

I cannot tell a lie.

I am mad, wild about you.

You are the whole world to me.

You are the sun and the moon and the stars.

You are everything I ever dreamed about or wanted or desired or hoped for all my life.

You are tender and warm and sweet and nice and you are dynamic.

If there was only one man left on the earth, I would pray it would be you.

> *Forever,*
> Patty R.
> England

☆ ☆ ☆

Dearly beloved Elvis,

Could you please come to Milwaukee some day and sing for us?

You have thousands of loyal and true fans in Milwaukee.

Milwaukee is a nice city and if you came to sing in Milwaukee, you would get a royal welcome as if you were a king.

I know you are very busy, but if you could find time to come to Milwaukee, all of your fans in Milwaukee would have the thrill of seeing you in the flesh instead of just on television or the movies.

Maybe you could come to Milwaukee and just sing one song.

That would only take a few minutes.

> *Your Milwaukee fan,*
> Raymond
> Milwaukee

Dear Elvis,

The lyrics for your songs are the most romantic words on earth.

They are more beautiful than Shakespeare or Robert Browning or Shelley or Keats.

The lyrics for your songs say things that nobody has ever said before.

They are filled with meaning and emotion and sincerity.

There have never been words like them before and each word and sentence means more to me than anything else.

I could sit and listen to the lyrics of your songs all day.

They are the greatest words in the English language.

> *Love forever,*
> Beth K.
> Chicago

☆ ☆ ☆

Dear Elvis,

Do you like girls who wear lipstick and much makeup?

My girl friend Stephanie, says that you probably like girls who have a natural beauty and do not have to smear their face with mess to look beautiful.

Is this true?

I hope because I do not wear much makeup.

It is not because I have a natural beauty.

It is because I have an allergy to makeup and when I put makeup, I have a rash.

> *Your fan,*
> Caroline L.
> France

Dearest Elvis,

Must you pay money to have your records?

I suppose you can have free your own records.

If I can have free Elvis Presley records, I will have every Elvis Presley record that was made.

I will pile them in my room until there was not any room for anything else in my room except me and my stereo.

I will listen to my Elvis records every second, every minute, every day of every week, for the rest of my life, forever, forever, forever.

Your love,
Madeleine Z.
France

☆ ☆ ☆

Dear Elvis Presley,

What do you think you would be if you were not a famous singer?

Do you think that maybe you would be a priest or maybe a dentist?

I am happy you became a singer.

Of course, you can help many people if you are a priest or a dentist, but a priest or a dentist cannot make a record or a movie that will make happy millions of people in the United States, Europe, South America and Japan.

You can always find a nice priest and a good dentist, but you can never find another Elvis Presley.

Your fan,
Armando B.
Argentina

For Elvis:

A world without Elvis,
Is a world without sun.
A world without Elvis,
Is no world at all.
A world without Elvis,
Is a world without seasons.
A world without Elvis,
Is a world without stars above.
A world without Elvis,
Is a world without love.

Megan K.
Ireland

Darling Elvis,

I put your picture on my pillow so that every night before I sleep I am very close to you.

I was used to have trouble sleeping and sometimes it will take me a long time before I sleep but not any more.

Ever since I have put your picture on my pillow, I sleep immediately and I have sweet, sweet dreams for the night.

You are better than any thing for sleep.

Love and kisses,
Gloria M.
Spain

Dearest Elvis Presley,

This letter comes from my heart.

It is a sincere letter and one I have been thinking about writing for a long, long time, but I never had the courage to sit down and write to you before.

What I wanted to say is this:

I think your music is wonderful. I get goose pimples every time I hear your marvelous voice. Sometimes when I hear you sing, I imagine that you are singing just to me, but of course I know that really isn't true.

I know that you have millions of other fans and you are singing to them too.

Even if you are not singing to me alone, I can go on dreaming and hoping that perhaps someday soon you will sing just for me.

When that happens, it will be the greatest day for me—even greater than the day I was born.

Love and kisses,
Paula G.
England

Dear beloved Elvis,

Roses are red
Violets are blue
Sugar is sweet
But not as sweet as you.

A love poem from,
Arlene C.
U.S.A.

Dear Elvis,

I wish you are my boyfriend, not the bad boyfriend I have.

My boyfriend's name is Luciano and he is fourteen years. He is OK, but he has braces on his teeth and some times his shirt is dirty and his pants are ripped.

I love Luciano, but I am not sure I really like him.

If I have a boyfriend like you, it will be good because with a boyfriend like Elvis Presley, I will have a boyfriend that I like and I love.

> *Your*
> Eleanora M.
> Italy

P.S. Luciano cannot sing.

Elvis, my love,

We are planning a party at my house and you are the guest of honor.

All the twenty-five members of our Elvis Presley Fan Club will be there and we hope you will be able to come too because you are the guest of honor, and if the guest of honor doesn't come, then the party will not be so good.

Please RSVP as soon as possible because we have to order the cake for the party and if you don't come, then we will have wasted $6.85 on a chocolate cake.

> *Your fan,*
> Gwen G.
> Tucson

Dear Elvis Presley,

Did you ever go to acting school or are you a natural born actor?

I have watched you in the movies in your pictures like *King Creole, Wild in the Country* and *Fun in Acapulco* and I think you are a great actor.

Someday you will win an Academy Award for your acting.

The only reason you haven't won an Academy Award so far is that the other actors are too jealous of you.

They are jealous because you are a great actor and a great singer and that is a dynamite combination.

Maybe if Robert Redford or Paul Newman could sing, they wouldn't be so jealous of you.

> *Love,*
> Aileen G.
> Dayton

Dear Elvis Presley,

Do you need somebody to take care of you when you are traveling from city to city for your concerts?

Somebody who can pack your suitcase, wash your clothes, shine your shoes, pick out your tie, shirt and suit?

I would like that somebody to be me.

I would take very good care of you because I am the motherly type.

> *Love,*
> Bernice W.
> Topeka

Dearest Elvis,

Why do you not make more movies?

You do not make enough movies.

The last Elvis Presley movie I have seen was two years since and I have not seen a movie since two years.

It is not worth going to the movies if I cannot see my Elvis.

If you stopped making records, I do not know what I will do because if I have not Elvis Presley records to listen to, I will put my stereo in the attic.

You see, dear Elvis, without you in the movies or in records, life is not be worth living.

I need Elvis to live like I need the sun, the moon, the stars, the air, and the sky.

You are my world.

All my love,
Irina M.
The Netherlands

☆ ☆ ☆

To my one and only Elvis,

I can climb the highest mountain
I can swim the furthest sea.
But I will never find anyone
Who means as much to me.

Alice F.
France

☆ ☆ ☆

Dear Elvis!

I think the record jackets for your record albums are works of art. They are beautiful.

Whenever I buy one of your albums, I take the record out of the jacket and then I frame the record jacket.

All over my room, there are framed Elvis Presley jackets.

I have them over my bed and over my stereo and over the little box where my dog, Charlie, sleeps.

I have more than twenty-three Elvis Presley record jackets framed and hanging on my walls and my room looks like a museum.

I hope you don't make too many more albums, Elvis.

It isn't that I don't want any more Elvis Presley records. It's just that if you make many more albums, I'll have to get a new room.

Your loyal fan,
Seth F.
Cold Spring
Harbor

☆ ☆ ☆

Dearly beloved Elvis Presley,

Whenever I am in church I say a special prayer for you.

I pray that you will have the same happiness that you have brought to all of your fans all over the world.

I hope my prayers are answered because I want you to be very happy, Elvis.

It would make me sad to think that you were ever sad, Elvis.

If you are ever sad, why don't you call me on the telephone and I will cheer you up by telling you a joke or playing one of your own records for you.

I don't have my own telephone so when you call me on the telephone and my mother answers the phone, just tell her you are a friend of mine.

Your loving fan,
Irma B.
U.S.A.

☆ ☆ ☆

☆ ☆ ☆

My darling, dearest, delicious Elvis,

You turn me.

It is not your records like "I Want You, I Love You" or "Too Much" or "All Shook Up" that turns me.

What really turns me is the look in your eyes and how you swing your hips when you sing on the stage or in the movies.

Something else turns me and that is your personality.

You are a very sweet, nice person and you are not conceited like some other superstars.

If I had to choose any body in the world to turn me, I will choose you.

Love from me,
Anna M.
Poland

☆ ☆ ☆

Dearest Elvis,

Sometimes when I listen to your records, I can't believe I am really listening to you.

When I listen to your records, it is as if I am listening to a magic voice that is taking me to far off romantic places.

Yesterday I listened to "Hound Dog" and I thought I was in beautiful Hawaii and today I listened to "Love Me Tender" and I imagined I was in India.

Tomorrow I will listen to another Elvis record and your magic voice will take me to some other romantic place.

I don't know yet where it will be, but I know that Elvis Presley is my magic carpet to the wonderful world of beautiful places.

Love and kisses,
Sylvia M.
U.S.A.

Dear Elvis,

I wish I was a great artist or poet so that I can express my inner feelings about you.

Alas, I am not an artist or a poet. I am another teenager who has a mad love for you, Elvis—one of your millions of teenager fans who can not truly express what you and your music mean.

Perhaps some day I will be an artist or a poet and the words will come more easy.

But now all I can say is I love you.

It is not poetry, but it comes from my heart.

> *Love,*
> Sonja O.
> Russia

To dear Elvis,

You are more popular in my country than the Queen.

You could be the King of England if you wanted to be.

> *Your loyal fan,*
> Gwen C.
> London

Beloved Elvis Presley,

    Elvis is the king,
Now and forever.
Elvis is the king,
In good or stormy weather.
Elvis is the king,
And that is sure.
He is loved by all,
The rich and the poor.
Elvis is the king,
Forever and a day.
Elvis is the king,
That is all there is to say!

Your loving fan,
Olga M.
Poland

Dear Elvis,

    I went to one of your shows in Las Vegas and I almost fainted.

    I couldn't believe that I was actually seeing you in the flesh.

    All my life, I had dreamed of seeing Elvis Presley in the flesh, but I never really believed it would really happen.

    Gosh you looked fantastic in person. I never really thought anybody could look so great in person until I saw you.

    I hope I can see you in person again in Las Vegas.

    I want to see if you look as fantastic in the flesh the second time as you did the first.

Ray W.
Hawaii

Dear Elvis,

Often I cry when I listen to your records, even though the records aren't sad.

I do not know the reason I cry when I listen to your records.

Maybe it is because your records make me so happy that I am crying because I am so happy.

I think there is not anything wrong about crying when I listen to your records but sometimes they get wet.

> *All my love,*
> Juanita L.
> Mexico

☆ ☆ ☆

Dear Elvis,

Do you think you could dedicate a record to me?

I am one of your loyal and true fans and it would be the greatest honor that ever happened to me if you would dedicate a record to me.

I know many of your other fans have probably made the same request and if you can't dedicate a record to me, I will understand.

I will still be an Elvis Presley fan even if the answer is no.

Richard ———— is not a fair weather fan.

When he became an Elvis Presley fan, it was forever.

> *Sincerely,*
> Richard S.
> U.S.A.

Dearest Elvis Presley,

    I wanted to say,
In the best possible way,
What you mean in my home,
So that is why I wrote this poem.
It is my simple way of saying to you,
That without your music I don't know what I
    would do.

                               Forever my love,
                               Alicia G.
                               Scotland

To my one and only Elvis,

    I am sending you a lock of my hair.
    Can you please send me a lock of your hair in
return?

                               Your adoring fan,
                               Sanai G.
                               Japan

P.S. If you cannot spare a lock of your hair, I will
understand.
P.P.S. I have plenty of hair.

☆ ☆ ☆

Dear Elvis,

I have joined an Elvis Presley Fan Club so I can be with other kids who feel about you how I do. But I have left the Elvis Presley Fan Club when I felt that the other girls in the Elvis Presley Fan Club were not as in love with Elvis Presley as me.

It is true the other girls in the Elvis Presley Fan Club like Elvis, and many love Elvis, but no one of them were really mad, wild, crazy about Elvis how I am.

I will look for another Elvis Presley Fan Club where the members are mad about Elvis how I am.

If I cannot find such Elvis Presley Fan Club then I will begin my own.

I want an Elvis Presley Fan Club which is the best Elvis Presley Fan Club in the whole world.

Your loyal fan,
Kare M.
Sweden

☆ ☆ ☆

☆ ☆ ☆

Dear Elvis, my love,

I will climb the highest mountain and swim the deepest sea for you.

I will sacrifice all my possessions for you.

I will dedicate my life for your happiness.

I will protect you and do all to make you the happiest man on earth now and in all the days of the glorious future.

I will do all this and what do I ask in return?

Nothing, nothing.

To know that I bring you some happiness, is enough for me. Just to know that, perhaps, I bring a smile to your face.

I pray to God that I can do this for you and I know that God will answer my prayers because, dear Elvis, God wants you to be happy too.

All my fondness,
Hilda R.
Germany

☆ ☆ ☆

Dearest Elvis,

I know that it is hopeless for me thinking you could ever have interest in me when you have all the beautiful women you meet every day all over the world.

What do I offer you can't find in Hollywood or another glamorous city?

I am not a raving beauty or glamour girl, but I do offer some things.

1. I am very good cook. You will love the lasagna.

2. I am good housekeeper and very tidy. Not untidy like many girls I know.

3. I am gentle person and I am very good to children and dogs and cats.

4. I have good sense of humor and I know some good jokes.

5. I dress good and I do not dress in jeans all day.

6. I am not genius, but many say I am very clever (especially Mama and Papa).

7. I do not spend much money, but I am not cheap.

8. I have good complexion and I do not wear too much makeup (only lipstick).

9. I am very clean and I take a bath once a day and two times a day in the summer.

10. I am not fat and I am not thin. I am right.

11. I have good teeth and I do not have holes because I do not eat candy and other sweets.

12. I am good conversationalist and I know many things, but I do not talk too often.

13. I am very romantic.

If you are interested in what I offer, please to telephone me. I am ready.

Fondly,
Rosa M.
Italy

Dear Elvis Presley,

I collect things that are worn by the stars.

Do you think you can send me something?

It must not have to be anything very valuable.

Maybe you can send me a shoe lace or a hand-kerchief or a button from an old shirt.

What you can send me, I will cherish and keep safe in a box under the bed.

I have fifteen buttons from fifteen different stars and I have not lost one button.

Oddvin
Norway

☆ ☆ ☆

Dear Elvis,

I can't believe that I actually saw you in person last night.

It was almost too good to be true.

Imagine me, Brenda ———, only ten feet away from Elvis Presley!

I thought I would die, but I didn't. Because if I was dead, I wouldn't be able to write you this letter.

You looked fantastic in person, Elvis.

If all of your fans could see you in person, they would know as I do that the real Elvis Presley is 1,000 percent more exciting in person than he is in the movies or on television.

You should appear in person more often, Elvis, because when you do you prove to the world that there is only one Elvis Presley and there will never be another for a million years, even if they try to invent one like they did the Atomic Bomb.

Your fan,
Brenda S.
Canada

☆ ☆ ☆

Dear Elvis,

What is your favorite color?

Someday, sometime, somewhere, if my prayers are answered, you and I will meet, Elvis, and I want to look pretty and nice for you so that is why I want to know your favorite color so when we will meet I can wear your favorite color.

If I must go to buy a new dress so I can wear your favorite color, I will do no matter how it costs.

Usually I wear only jeans and a blouse or sweater, but I want to look special when I will meet you.

I do not care what you are wearing when we meet, Elvis.

Elvis, you will look beautiful in anything.

Love,
Wanda M.
Norway